MEN, WOMEN
AND WEDLOCK

Looking for Trouble.

MEN, WOMEN
AND WEDLOCK

A CONFESSION BOOK OF BORROWINGS FROM VARIOUS CLASSICS, WITH SOME MODERN INSTANCES BY "CELT"

LONDON
A & C Black
1910

Acknowledgment and thanks are due to the "Mary Evans Picture Library," by whose courtesy the illustrations in this book have been reproduced.

A WORD
THE WISE

If you are not entertained by the plagiarisms in the following pages, blame Madame de Staël, Ninon de L'Enclos, Chesterfield, Rousseau, Pascal, Ben Jonson, Balzac, La Fontaine, Voltaire, Steele, Æschylus, Congreve, Anonymous, or any others you may have a grudge against. Being a lover of peace and having a horror of bloodshed, so far as personally concerned, I have thought it wise to take no visible credit for my own contributions.

You are hereby invited to get your friends to choose half a dozen (more or less) of the truths that lie herein, and, on one of the blank pages left for the purpose, transcribe the epigrams by number, and sign their names underneath, thus:—

31, 61, 91, 121, 151, 181.

Celt

Believe me, the result will afford you an excellent guide to their characters.

LONDON, *December*, 1910.

A fair exchange is no robbery

MEN, WOMEN
AND WEDLOCK

1.

There is at least one woman in the world for every man in the world to think the world of.

2.

Many people are busy in the present making a past for the future.

3.

Listening, with most of us, is waiting till the other person has finished.

4.

Many a man is out of work because there is no work in him.

5.

Never take a better half unless you are sure of better quarters.

6.

Women go to the theatre to see what women in the stalls have on; men to see what women on the stage have off.

7.

It takes a lot of polish to enable a man to shine in society.

8.

There is at least one good point about being married : while you are, you can't be so foolish again.

9.

If women were less extravagant men would be more honest.

10.

It is not easy to be a widow. She has to resume all the modesty of girlhood without being allowed even to feign ignorance.

11.

The fool and his money are what keep the rest of us from starving to death.

12.

Women speak easily of platonic love; yet there is not a frill or a ribbon about them that is not meant to drive platonism from men's hearts.

13.

We never hear the best things that are said about us. We are dead by then.

14.

If men knew all that women think, they would be twenty times more audacious.

15.

All women want to think they are misunderstood; all men want to think they understand.

16.

Many a man has fallen in love with a peach only to discover that Fate has handed him a lemon.

17.

All women's love is "touching," but some tastes are more expensive than others.

18.

Even the dreamer attracts attention—when he snores.

19.

You never hear married men say that figures cannot lie. They know the naked truth.

20.

A good complexion on the fact is worth two at the chemist's.

21.

The man who cuts off his nose to spite his face can't very well blow about it.

22.

Women always love colour better than form, rhetoric better than logic, priestcraft better than philosophy, and flourishes better than figures.

23.

If marriages are made in heaven, then how few there seem to be with friends there.

24.

Love is blind, they say. That perhaps is why he depends so largely on the sense of touch.

25.

Many a man is credited with being patient when he is merely too lazy to register a kick.

26.

Men always notice what a woman's petticoat is like—when they see it; but her outer garments, never.

27.

Saying the right thing at the right time is equivalent to keeping your mouth shut when you have nothing to say.

28.

When a man is looking for trouble he'll find plenty to help him in the search.

29.

A girl must be very, very intellectual if she can't tell you what another girl had on.

30.

Man wears clothes as a defence; woman for the purpose of attack.

31.

If a girl remains single till her ideal man comes along, the chances are that her maiden name will adorn a tombstone.

32.

It is not absence, but abstinence, that makes the heart grow fonder.

33.

The craze for antiques notwithstanding, few men are eager to snap up the old maid.

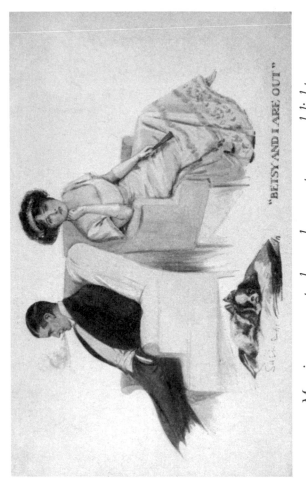

"BETSY AND I ARE OUT"

Marriage cannot always be sweetness and light

34.

When a woman begins to feel happy, she begins to feel miserable for fear such happiness is too good to last.

35.

When a man relates that he has just got married it will puzzle you to know whether he wants congratulation or sympathy.

36.

Some people never seem to weary in their efforts to make other people so.

37.

The best way to make your opinions respected is to keep them to yourself.

38.

No matter how long a woman has been in the market she still likes to be quoted at about 25.

39.

Many men find it the most difficult thing in life to eliminate politics from their patriotism.

40.

Ladies, like soldiers, must keep their powder dry if they would escape missing fire.

41.

There's no time like the pleasant.

42.

Some men waste all their energy trying to impress us with the fact that something ought to be done.

43.

Most hair tonics, so called, raise a lot more hope than hair.

44.

Few men reach fifty without being grateful they didn't get the woman they wanted.

45.

Many a man's good intentions are due to the headache next morning.

46.

Lots of women marry for the purpose of securing a listener who can't get away.

47.

Don't make love to a girl in a hammock; you may both fall out.

48.

A philosopher has divided mankind into two classes: those who are and those who are not found out. He means married and single, no doubt.

49.

Man proposes; woman makes him stick to it.

50.

A most serious case is a doctor without one.

51.

The worst fault about some people is that they haven't any.

52.

Flattery may be counterfeit, but it frequently passes where truth would not.

53.

If you are puzzled how to stop your wife being jealous without cause, give her cause.

54.

The average man includes his cigar bills in the cost of supporting his family.

55.

Most of the things we wish for are about as useful as a lead shilling.

56.

Nothing pleases a large woman more than to have a man call her a dear little girl.

57.

Love and logic are not on speaking terms.

58.

Some women wear combs to hold their hair up; others to hold it on.

59.

The more intelligent a girl is the easier is it for her to remain single.

60.

It's a waste of time to find fault with yourself; there are so many ready to do it for you.

61.

Never mix your women.

62.

Before marriage, woman is all bait; after it, all hook.

63.

It's not the fancy dress that makes the fool.

64.

A few are anxious to earn money; most are merely anxious to get it.

65.

When Nature forgets to make a fool of a man it gives some woman a chance.

66.

A man who can write a convincing love letter ought to be able to make money as a novelist.

67.

Woman would be more charming if one could fall into her arms without falling into her hands.

68.

Men are generally regular in their habits— when they are bad habits.

*Many a girl's success on the river
of life lies in looking pretty and
paddling her own canoe*

69.

A man never realises how many friends he has till he doesn't need them.

70.

There are just two kinds of women in the world: the ones you must kiss and the ones you daren't.

71.

Many a man who demands justice would whine for mercy if he got it.

72.

Some girls are so proper that one wonders how they can think of going on a wedding trip without a chaperon.

73.

A man who can joke with his wife about her dressmaker's bill must have a keen sense of humour.

74.

Don't look for trouble unless you know what to do with it when you find it.

75.

Marriage isn't always a failure. Moreover there is always a fighting chance.

76.

Speaking of office-holders, few die and all are too patriotic to resign.

77.

If marriage is a lottery then alimony must be a sort of gambling debt.

78.

The law has no penalty for stealing a heart. The punishment of having it left on your hands is enough.

79.

Somehow or other marriage doesn't seem nearly so important to a woman—when she has accomplished it.

80.

Matches are made in heaven—perhaps; but they are certainly sold on earth.

81.

Convince a woman that she is getting a bargain, and she will pay anything.

82.

Modesty in woman is a virtue most deserving, since men do all they can to cure her of it.

83.

Women are too often apt to see the defects of a man of talent and the merits of a fool.

84.

Women envy men their vices not because they are less vicious but because Fashion has put a restraint on them.

85.

The society of women endangers men's morals and refines their manners.

86.

When a man says he is wedded to his art, then some woman is to be congratulated on her escape.

87.

There is no mortification like that of the woman who gets a new dress to wear at a party and then isn't invited.

88.

Often a man swears without meaning it; just as often a woman means it without swearing.

89.

Why should man, who is strong, always get the best of it, and be forgiven so much; while woman, who is weak, gets the worst of it and is forgiven so little?

90.

Before you give a man advice it is advisable to find out the kind he wants.

91.

It is no rare thing for a woman to drown her honour in the clear water of diamonds.

92.

A woman often makes a fool of herself because it is expected of her. A man does so because he can't help himself.

93.

It is very sad when a man is thrown on his own resources and finds he hasn't any.

94.

Woman is an overgrown child that one amuses with toys, intoxicates with flattery, and seduces with promises.

95.

There never will be universal peace; people always will get married.

96.

There are no women to whom virtue comes easier than those who possess no attractions.

97.

The average woman can't refrain from chuckling when her best friend makes a fool of herself.

98.

God invented the coquette about the same time that he produced the fool.

99.

A good method of having your way if you are a married man is to find out your wife's opinion, and then agree with her.

100.

A man may have heart enough to love two women at the same time; but he certainly ought to have brains enough not to try it.

101.

The slow girl often gets soonest to the altar.

102.

He who is disappointed in love doesn't run so much risk of being disappointed in marriage.

103.

Riches have wings, but they are probably not the kind of wings that are fashionable in heaven.

Working their way up

104.

The woman who dresses better than her friends will never be popular with them.

105.

Why have women usually more good sense than men? Because they cannot reason wrong. They do not reason at all.

106.

Plenty of women never seem to understand why their husbands should need any spending money.

107.

Let every man pray that the woman he loves may never form an accurate estimate of him.

108.

Ignorance at the right time is better than knowledge at the wrong time.

109.

There are some women who think virtue was given them as claws were given to cats—to do nothing but scratch with.

110.

At a certain age a woman begins to worry for fear she won't get married, and a man for fear he will.

111.

A woman can love only one man at a time. It is for the husband just to see that he is that man.

112.

The resistance of a woman is more frequently a proof of her experience than of her virtue.

113.

Love means the association of two beings for the benefit of one.

114.

A quick lunch maketh a slow liver.

115.

Only a few can have their faces on coins. Still, most people are content to get their hands on them.

116.

When a man says he has a wife, you can take it that in reality a wife has him.

117.

There are three things, lovable and beautiful, about when men never quite agree. They are painting, music and woman.

118.

A man never quite realises how little he knows about women till he marries one.

119.

The young fellow who feels that he is destined to set the world on fire never seems to alarm the insurance companies.

120.

It is easier for a woman to defend her virtue against men than her reputation against women.

121.

Women ask if a man is discreet, just in the same way as men ask if a woman is pretty.

122.

To marry at sixty a beautiful girl of twenty is to imitate those foolish people who buy books to be read by their friends.

123.

We like our friends to be perfectly frank with us—about other people.

124.

A man may be rich enough to do as he pleases —provided he isn't married.

125.

There are people who could help more by giving less advice.

126.

The suitors for the hand of an heiress never trouble to ask for proof of her past virtue.

127.

The trouble with truth seems to be that most of us are too polite to tell it.

128.

Woman among savages is a beast of burden; in Asia she is a piece of furniture; in Europe she is a spoiled child.

129.

The woman who throws herself at a man's head will soon find her place at his feet.

130.

The average theatre audience likes to be electrified, but it prefers to be shocked.

131.

He who takes an eel by the tail or a woman at her word soon finds he holds nothing.

132.

The man who puts up a good front often does so to compensate for his lack of backing.

133.

Sometimes a woman wishes she were a man so that she might break the hearts of other women.

134.

Women give themselves to God when Satan wants nothing more to do with them.

135.

The man who inscribes himself "your humble servant" or "yours obediently" thoroughly deserves to be made a mat of.

136.

Have you ever noticed that the women who spoil paper with essays on how to choose a husband are all old maids?

137.

A dumb woman must certainly be classed as one of the wonders of the world.

138.

Wives are young men's mistresses and old men's nurses.

Marriage is always surprising

139.

It is difficult for a woman to keep a secret; and there are too many men who show themselves no better than women.

140.

Some fellows are prompted to look for work merely out of idle curiosity.

141.

Women, deceived by men, want to marry them. What more thorough form of revenge could they have than that?

142.

It is too bad that people can't get into heaven with their tombstone inscriptions as passports.

143.

Every man should know his duty—even if only so as to recognise it in time to dodge.

144.

A woman is seldom tenderer to a man than immediately after she has deceived him.

145.

A foolish woman believes everything her husband tells her. A wise woman merely pretends to.

146.

The complaint of not a few women against their husbands is that the latter give them no ground for complaint.

147.

Man without woman is head without body; woman without man is body without head.

148.

To love is to admire with the heart; to admire is to love with the mind.

149.

Why do women reserve praise of their husbands till they become widows? Probably to use it in stormy moments as a weapon against the second mate.

150.

The highest mark of esteem a woman can give a man is to ask his friendship, and the most signal, proof of her indifference is to offer him hers.

151.

The secret of youthful looks in an aged face is easy shoes, an easy purse, easy corsets and an easy conscience.

152.

Why should you worry on a voyage if the ship goes down? It isn't yours.

153.

If Cleopatra's nose had been shorter the face of the whole world would have been changed.

154.

A beautiful woman is the paradise of the eyes, the hell of the soul and the purgatory of the purse.

155.

There's one thing about wild oats: they never fail to grow.

156.

It sometimes looks as though a wise providence had created woman so that man might always blame her for his defects and misfortunes.

157.

It is what a woman suspects that generally shocks her most.

158.

No woman who is entirely good, in the ordinary sense of the word, gets a man's most fervent, passionate love.

159.

Where a secret is concerned a woman makes every word tell.

160.

Women like brave men, but they adore audacious ones.

161.

Brevity is the soul of wit. That probably is why so few preachers are witty.

162.

What's the good of a cook-book when it doesn't tell you how to keep a cook.

163.

Of one thing only can you be sure in woman; she will not come to life again when she is dead.

164.

A man can keep another's secret better than his own; a woman, on the contrary, keeps her secret though she tells all others.

165.

I am glad I am not a man, as I should be obliged to marry a woman.

166.

In spite of themselves some men seem to get on—and some to get off.

167.

The heartache of many a widow has been tempered by the reflection that she looks her best in black.

168.

The man whose wife takes in washing usually knows exactly how the country should be governed.

169.

Women, cats and birds are the creatures that waste most time on their toilet. And a woman is usually either a cat or a duck, isn't she?

170.

About the only library that a newly married couple requires consists of a cheque-book and a cook-book.

171.

Man argues that woman should not be trusted too far; woman feels that man cannot be trusted too near.

172.

An innocent lie never hurts so much as a malicious truth.

173.

The office-holder always believes that one good term deserves another.

*Older men often possess new
diamonds*

174.

Many a married man feels like a hypocrite when he is congratulating a newly married couple.

175.

The lazy man naturally resents being told to go to the devil, since Satan always finds some work for idle hands to do.

176.

In buying a horse and in taking a wife, shut your eyes tight and commend yourself to God.— *Tuscan proverb.*

177.

Women swallow at one mouthful the lie that flatters, and drink drop by drop the truth that is bitter.

178.

The patriot is frequently the man who always takes off his hat to the flag and always dodges his taxes.

179.

There are plenty of Dick Turpins in society of to-day. Their motto is "Your money or your wife."

180.

In this advanced century a girl of sixteen knows as much as her mother, and enjoys her knowledge much more.

181.

A young girl should make the most of her birthdays, for after she gets a little older she won't have any.

182.

A beautiful woman should be as a hidden treasure. Whoso discovers her would do well not to brag about it.

183.

A warm friend is the kind of one to freeze on to.

184.

A woman may not be able to recall just when her husband proposed; but she can always remember what dress she had on at the time.

185.

Most men of prominence are highly esteemed by those who don't know them.

186.

No woman feels that she is old enough to have her age guessed at.

187.

When a man is known as a confirmed bachelor it means that a great many girls have acted as priests at his confirmation.

188.

A woman may either make a fool of a fellow or help him to make one of himself.

189.

The listener who wants to hear good of herself generally has to talk into a phonograph first.

190.

The world is slow to recognise genius. But you must remember that the world gets precious little practice in that line.

191.

A safe bet is the one you were going to make —and didn't.

192.

It may be possible to love two women at one time. But not if they know it.

193.

Some people think they are philosophers because they manage to laugh at other people's misery.

194.

Faint heart ne'er won fair lady. Nor did it ever escape the clutches of one.

195.

A bachelor seeks a wife to avoid solitude; a married man seeks society to avoid a *tête-à-tête*.

196.

Never explain to a woman. If you want to convince her when you say "I love you," don't you be fool enough to add "You're such a jolly good sort."

197.

The wife who comes down to breakfast with her hair anyhow starts her husband on the road to some other breakfast-table.

198.

It is hard to make something out of nothing, but a bathing-dress goes far towards accomplishment.

199.

The man who is backward at proposing doesn't necessarily make a meek husband.

200.

When Eve ate the apple she was naked. Often as one looks upon her dancing daughters of to-day one is tempted to think that another bite would be of service to them.

201.

One must have loved a woman of knowledge and erudition in order to comprehend what happiness there is in loving a fool.

202.

Many a man's wife nowadays is too rich to agree with him.

203.

The worst thing about looking for trouble is that we generally run against someone who is willing to accommodate us.

204.

It is all very well to toe the mark—except when we happen to be the mark.

205.

It is bad enough to be poor, bad enough to be plain. But to be both at once is more than any woman ought to be called upon to bear.

206.

Most of us believe in doing to others as we would have them do to us. But we generally wait for them to do it first.

207.

The only way to keep kindness is to keep it in circulation.

208.

Dress doesn't necessarily make the woman. You can't always tell a typist by her ribbons.

209.

Never bluntly call a man a liar. Break the news gently. It is better for yourself.

210.

The collection-plate may get the pennies and the shillings, but the box-office usually gets the gold.

211.

When you hear a pretty girl sing "I would I were an angel bright," it doesn't signify that she is in any hurry about it.

212.

Darwin notwithstanding, the sons of some of our newly-rich make it obvious that the ape is descended from man.

213.

We never seem to see anything to laugh at in the bad grammar of people who pay us compliments.

214.

"All the world loves a lover": especially the jeweller, the florist, and the confectioner.

215.

Orpheus went to hell to find his wife. How many widowers would not even go to heaven to find theirs!

216.

Woman was taken from the side of a man. It is for the mutual happiness of both that she is ever fond of her birthplace.

217.

There is a magic in Duty which sustains judges, inflames warriors, and cools the married.

218.

Some girls marry well; others happily.

219.

Many a girl's idea of doing good in the world is to marry a man to reform him.

220.

It is easy to find a lover and to retain a friend. What is difficult is to retain the lover and find the friend.

221.

One half the world that gets along doesn't know how the other half gets short.

222.

A man never can do two things well at the same time, if being in love is one of them.

223.

Some folk get such swollen heads from their religion that their haloes won't fit them when they get to heaven.

224.

The woman who looks as though she had a secret sorrow is always interesting till she tries to tell it you.

225.

When a fellow tells a girl he will love her always, sometimes both of them are young enough to believe it.

226.

We should all try to endure our own troubles with the same admirable fortitude that has helped us to endure those of our friends.

227.

There are two ways by which a woman can get even with a man. One way is to marry him; the other is not to.

228.

Nature does not always distribute her gifts with discretion. There is the man with whiskers and a bald head, for instance.

229.

Even the introduction of a few motor-cars into a musical comedy does not entirely eliminate horse-play.

230.

How many women would laugh at the funerals of their husbands if it were not the custom to cry!

231.

Men say that knowledge is power. Women know that dress is power.

232.

The present-day philosopher is not necessarily a college man. Frequently he is merely a fellow who preaches what he doesn't practice.

233.

There are lots of people who live according to their convictions. But they are chiefly in gaol.

Living Dangerously

Available from all reputable booksellers

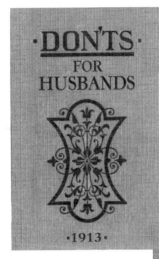

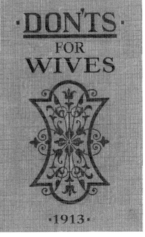

Originally published 1910
Republished 2009 by A&C Black Publishers Limited
Copyright © A&C Black, 2009
36 Soho Square, London, W1D 3QY
www.acblack.com

ISBN 9781408113790

A CIP catalogue record for this book is available from the British
Library.

Printed by WKT Company Ltd, China